SCIENCE EXPLORER

ECOSYSTEMS

SUPER COOL
SCIENCE
EXPERIMENTS:
ECOSYSTEMS

by Matt Mullins

CHERRY LAKE PUBLISHING • ANN ARBOR, MICHIGAN

CHERRY
LAKE
Publishing

A NOTE TO PARENTS AND TEACHERS: Please review the instructions for these experiments before your children do them. Be sure to help them with any experiments you do not think they can safely conduct on their own.

A NOTE TO KIDS: Be sure to ask an adult for help with these experiments when you need it. Always put your safety first!

Published in the United States of America by
Cherry Lake Publishing
Ann Arbor, Michigan
www.cherrylakepublishing.com

Content Editor: Robert Wolffe, EdD,
Professor of Teacher Education,
Bradley University, Peoria, Illinois

Book design and illustration: The Design Lab

Photo Credits: Cover and page 1, ©Thomas Barrat, used under license from Shutterstock, Inc.; page 5, ©blickwinkel/Alamy; page 8, ©Rich Carey, used under license from Shutterstock, Inc.; page 16, ©silver-john, used under license from Shutterstock, Inc.; page 19, ©WoodyStock/Alamy; page 20, ©iStockphoto.com/Acik; page 24, ©Maksym Gorpenyuk, used under license from Shutterstock, Inc.

Library of Congress Cataloging-in-Publication Data
Mullins, Matt.
  Super cool science experiments: Ecosystems / by Matt Mullins.
    p. cm.—(Science explorer)
  Includes index.
  ISBN-13: 978-1-60279-516-7   ISBN-10: 1-60279-516-9 (lib. bdg.)
  ISBN-13: 978-1-60279-595-2   ISBN-10: 1-60279-595-9 (pbk.)
1. Biotic communities—Experiments—Juvenile literature. I. Title.
II. Title: Ecosystems. III. Series.
  QH541.14.M85 2010
  577.078—dc22   2009004582

Cherry Lake Publishing would like to acknowledge the work of The Partnership for 21st Century Skills. Please visit www.21stcenturyskills.org for more information.

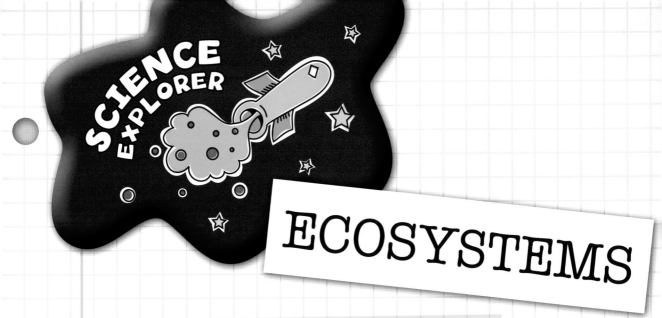

ECOSYSTEMS

TABLE OF CONTENTS

Nature's Communities

Animals and plants live together in ecosystems.

When you think of science, what comes to mind? Do you think of experts using lots of fancy and expensive equipment? Do you picture complicated formulas and confusing graphs?

All of these things can be part of science. But you can also do experiments with things you already have at home. It's easier than you might imagine! In this book, we'll learn how scientists think. We'll do that by running experiments about ecosystems. The best part? We'll have fun and learn many things along the way!

First Things First

There are many different ecosystems to explore.

An ecosystem is a network or community of living things and the environment they live in. Scientists learn by studying things very carefully. Scientists who study ecosystems watch how animals travel within them, how plants grow, and how water runs through the area. They discover which plants grow best in different regions. They examine how plants and animals from one ecosystem move into another.

Good scientists take notes on everything they discover. They write down their observations. Sometimes those observations lead scientists to ask new questions. With new questions in mind, they design experiments to find the answers.

When scientists design experiments, they must think very clearly. The way they think about problems is often called the scientific method. What is the scientific method? It's a step-by-step way of finding answers to specific questions. The steps don't always follow the same pattern. Sometimes scientists change their minds. The process often works something like this:

Scientific method

- **Step One:** A scientist gathers the facts and makes observations about one particular thing.
- **Step Two:** The scientist comes up with a question that is not answered by all the observations and facts.
- **Step Three:** The scientist creates a hypothesis. This is a statement of what the scientist thinks is probably the answer to the question.
- **Step Four:** The scientist tests the hypothesis. He or she designs an experiment to see whether the hypothesis is correct. The scientist does the experiment and writes down what happens.

- **Step Five:** The scientist draws a conclusion based on how the experiment turned out. The conclusion might be that the hypothesis is correct. Sometimes, though, the hypothesis is not correct. In that case, the scientist might develop a new hypothesis and another experiment.

In the following experiments, we'll see the scientific method in action. We'll gather some facts and observations about ecosystems and the life that thrives in them. For each experiment, we'll develop a question and a hypothesis. Next, we'll do an actual experiment to see if our hypothesis is correct. By the end of the experiment, we should know something new about ecosystems. Scientists, are you ready? Then let's get started!

Get ready to write down your observations!

Experiment #1 Diversity at the Borders

← Coral reefs are ocean ecosystems.

An ecological system is made up of an area and everything that's found in it—plants, animals, rocks, soil, air, and water. It's a community. Some of the life in this community is so tiny that you need a microscope to see it. There are forest ecosystems, ocean ecosystems, and many others. Every kind of region you can think of can be an ecosystem.

Studying ecosystems can be difficult because there are so many parts to study. One of the hardest things about studying an ecosystem is figuring out where one ecosystem ends and the next begins.

The place where one ecosystem runs into another is called an ecotone. What do you think might be living in the space where two ecosystems meet? Ecotones have plants and animals from each ecosystem that borders them. Could this mean that more types of wildlife live in an ecotone than the ecosystems that form it? Let's find out. Here is one hypothesis you might want to test: **Ecotones have more plants and animals than the ecosystems right next to them.**

Here's what you'll need:
- An ecotone, where two ecosystems meet
- A big ring (a hula hoop works great)
- A science notebook
- A pencil

Your parents or teachers can help you find an ecotone.

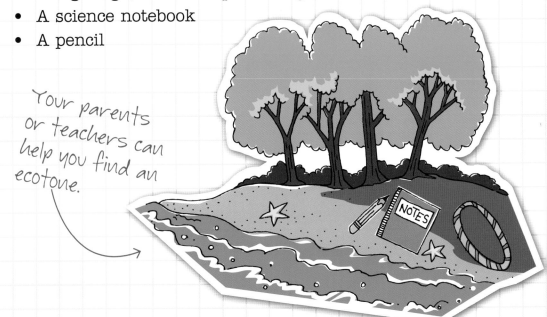

9

Instructions:

1. Find an ecotone near you. It can be a forest and a field, a pond and a grassland, or a prairie and a beach. Ask an adult to go with you. Go to the border of the ecosystems. Walk 15 steps into one of the ecosystems. Stop. Toss the ring down beside you.

2. Study what you see inside the ring. In your notebook, label one sheet "Ecosystem 1, Toss 1." Count how many different types of plants and animals you see. Count trees if they have branches overhead. Include birds that fly overhead and insects found in the soil. Write down all the numbers.

Write down what you see inside the ring.

3. Now toss the ring nearby. Record the number of different plants and animals you see on a new page, labeled "Ecosystem 1, Toss 2."

4. Return to the ecotone. Now walk 15 steps into the other ecosystem. Toss the ring down and record your findings on a sheet labeled "Ecosystem 2, Toss 1." Now toss the ring nearby and record your new results on a sheet labeled "Ecosystem 2, Toss 2."

5. Go back to the ecotone and toss the ring down there. Record the number of different plants and animals you find on a sheet labeled "Ecotone, Toss 1." Repeat the process nearby, and write down the results on a sheet labeled "Ecotone, Toss 2."

6. Analyze your data. Find the average number of different plants and animals in Ecosystem 1 by adding the two values you recorded and dividing by 2. Round your answer to the nearest whole number. Do the same for Ecosystem 2. Now calculate the value for the ecotone.

Conclusion:

What can you conclude from this experiment? On average, did you find more kinds of plants, animals, and insects in the ecotone than you did in either Ecosystem 1 or Ecosystem 2? Did you see plants and animals from both ecosystems in the ecotone?

Sometimes scientists use the words biome and ecosystem to mean the same thing. Biomes are groupings of plants and animals that extend across a large region. These areas feature different types of plants, animals, climates, and landscapes. The marine biome is one example. It includes the oceans of the world and the things that live in them. What other biomes can you think of?

Experiment #2
The Temperature Is Just Right

Airflow, water supply, and temperature are among the most important environmental factors in a healthy ecosystem. Why do some plants prefer one ecosystem and different plants prefer others? One way we can investigate this is by studying a creature common to many ecosystems. You might already have this organism in your kitchen: yeast. Yeast is a living thing that emits carbon dioxide gas when it feeds. The gas from yeast creates bubbles in bread as it rises.

Yeast, like other living things, requires just the right temperature to live and be active. Has your family ever baked a loaf of bread? Recipes often suggest dissolving the yeast in warm water. Why not use very hot or very cold water? This is a good question to think about. Here are three possible hypotheses to choose from:

Hypothesis #1: Yeast works best at lukewarm temperatures.

Hypothesis #2: Yeast works best at cold temperatures.

Hypothesis #3: Yeast works best at hot temperatures.

Here's what you'll need:
- 4 empty 12-ounce (354.9 milliliter) bottles
- A marker
- 4 tablespoons of sugar
- 4 tablespoons of baking yeast (active dry yeast)
- 4 Styrofoam cups
- A ½ cup measuring cup
- Ice cubes
- Thermometer
- A microwavable cup
- Microwave oven
- 4 balloons
- 4 rubber bands
- String
- Ruler
- Science notebook

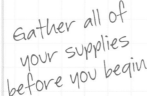

Gather all of your supplies before you begin.

Instructions:

1. Label the 4 bottles "A," "B," "C," and "D" with a marker. Place 1 tablespoon of sugar and 1 tablespoon of yeast in each bottle.
2. Label the 4 cups "A," "B," "C," and "D." Measure ½ cup of cool water, and pour it into cup A. Then add 1 ice cube.
3. Run warm tap water and check it with a thermometer until it reaches 70 degrees Fahrenheit (21.1 degrees Celsius). Measure ½ cup of the warm water, and pour it into cup B.
4. Run the tap water to 100°F (37.8°C). Measure ½ cup of the hot water, and pour that into cup C.
5. Pour ½ cup of water into a microwavable cup. Place it in the microwave, and heat it for 30 seconds. Have an adult help you check the temperature, reheating it if necessary, until the water reaches 150°F (65.6°C). Pour this heated water into cup D.
6. Record the temperatures of each cup of water in your notebook.

Make sure you label the bottles and cups.

Notes:
A:
B:
C:
D:

7. Pour the contents of cup A into bottle A. Swirl the bottle to mix the yeast, sugar, and water.
8. Stretch the open end of a balloon over the mouth of the bottle. Wrap a rubber band around the area where the balloon covers the bottle, to make a tight seal.
9. Do the same with cup B and bottle B, cup C and bottle C, and cup D and bottle D. Work at a quick but safe pace. You don't want the warm water samples to cool off too much before you finish.
10. Now measure the gas produced by the active yeast. Use a string and wrap it around the widest part of the balloon. Remove the string, and use a ruler to measure the length it took to reach around the balloon. Do this every 10 minutes for the next 30 minutes. Record these measurements.

Conclusion:
Which balloon expanded fastest? Which balloon expanded the least? Which the most? The yeast that produced the most gas was the most active at the temperature of its environment. This yeast inflated the balloon the most. So which temperature was best for the yeast? Yeast needs a little warmth, but water that is too hot or too cold can kill it. Does that fact help explain your results? Was your hypothesis correct? It doesn't matter if it wasn't. The experiment still helped you discover that certain living things have specific needs.

Experiment #3
Diversity: It's a Good Thing!

Most plants grow best when they get plenty of sunshine.

In an ecosystem where there is yeast, there are typically other living things, too. In a healthy, diverse ecosystem, plants and animals go about their lives. Their actions sometimes help other living things. Plants, for example, convert sunlight and rainfall into oxygen. That oxygen can then be used by animals.

Sometimes plants release gases that help other nearby plants. Green bananas release a gas called ethylene. Ethylene helps certain fruits ripen faster. Some fruits emit more ethylene than others. Apples release even more ethylene than bananas. With that in mind, think about a hypothesis. One possibility you might want to test is: **An apple works better than a banana at helping other bananas ripen faster.**

Here's what you'll need:
- 3 small brown paper bags
- A marker
- 1 soft, ripe apple
- 4 green, unripe bananas
- 1 soft, ripe banana
- A science notebook

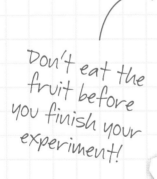

Don't eat the fruit before you finish your experiment!

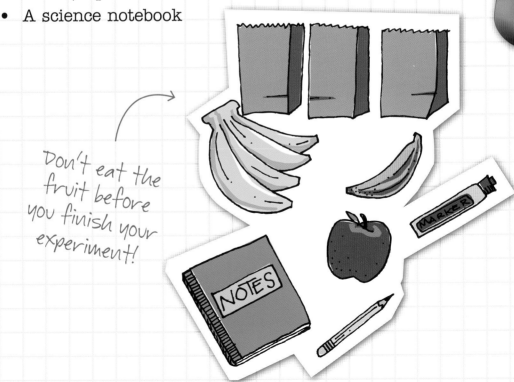

A is for apple!

Instructions:

1. Label the paper bags "A," "B," and "C" with the marker.
2. Place the apple and 1 unripe banana in bag A. Place the ripe banana and 1 unripe banana in bag B. Place 2 unripe bananas in bag C. Fold down the tops of the bags.
3. Move the bags to 3 locations around your house or school. The locations should have similar temperatures and receive the same amount of light.
4. Wait 2 days, and check the bags. In your notebook, write down how ripe the previously green bananas appear. Fold the bags closed again.
5. In 3 days, rate the bananas again. Write down your observations.
6. Wait 3 more days and rate the bananas a final time. Record your observations.

Conclusion:

Which unripe banana ripened fastest? Which ripened slowest? How well did the ripe apple, the ripe banana, and the unripe banana help the other bananas become more ripe? Your observations probably led you to conclude that the apple helped the banana ripen faster than another banana did. Though bananas and apples may not necessarily live in the same ecosystem in nature, they help demonstrate how fruits of one kind can help fruits of another. Diversity in an ecosystem helps the things that live in them thrive.

Have you ever seen bananas growing on a banana plant?

Experiment #4

Preventing Erosion

Bike traffic and erosion keep plants from growing on this path

Have you ever noticed any worn-down paths at the park? Rain that falls and drains away probably played a part in wearing down these paths. Wind and water can cause erosion by moving topsoil away and leaving behind dirt that isn't very good for growing plants.

Plants and soil need one another to stay in place. A healthy ecosystem resists erosion by keeping a good balance of plants and soil together. Let's see if we can explore this relationship with a simple experiment. Think about using plants that you might easily find. How about grass? Now think of a hypothesis that relates to grass and erosion. Here is one option: **Grass cover reduces erosion.**

Here's what you'll need:
- 2 rectangular baking pans of the same size
- Soil
- Grass seeds
- Water
- A thick book
- Water pitcher

You can find grass seed at garden shops or hardware stores.

Set up the experiment like this.

Instructions:

1. Fill each baking pan with soil.
2. In one pan, sprinkle grass seeds on the surface and press them into the soil.
3. In the other pan, press the dirt in like you did with the grass seeds, but don't add seeds.
4. Water each pan thoroughly, and place them in a window where they can get sunlight.
5. The next part of the experiment requires a little patience. Wait for the grass to sprout.
6. Once the grass is a few inches tall, place the book flat on your work surface. Now lean one end of each pan at an angle against an edge of the book. The pans should stand at an angle, kind of like slides on the playground.

7. The next part of the experiment may get a bit messy, so be sure you are working in an area that can be easily cleaned. Fill a pitcher with water. Pour the water into the pans from the top, one pan at a time.

Conclusion:

What does the water do in the pan with dry dirt? Does the water move a lot of the soil? How does the water behave in the grassy dirt? What does this tell us about how plants affect soil erosion?

Each year in the 1990s, the world lost growth in tropical rain forests equal to an area the size of Washington State. Most of this loss was due to human activity, including logging and clearing land for farming and housing. How might these activities cause serious problems involving soil erosion? Rain forests continue to get even smaller today. What impact do you think this has on rain forest ecosystems?

Experiment #5
Pollution and Plant Growth

Squirrels are just one kind of animal that spreads seeds around.

Soil is an important part of many ecosystems. Plants add nutrients to the soil when they die and rot. Animals spread seeds and nutrients when they eat and make waste. In a healthy ecosystem, plants and animals keep adding nutrients to the soil. But not everything humans add to an ecosystem necessarily helps it. Humans pollute air, water, and soil. Our cars drip oil that makes its way into waterways. We use pesticides that get carried by water into streams, lakes, and oceans.

This pollution makes it more difficult for ecosystems to thrive. Pollution affects the ways ecosystems support plants and animals, clean and filter water, and contribute oxygen to the atmosphere. Do you think even a little pollution can make growth difficult for sensitive seeds? That question is a good focus for our next experiment. Come up with a hypothesis. Or try testing this one: **A small amount of pollution prevents seeds from producing as well as they would without pollution.**

How can we cut down on pollution?

Here's what you'll need:
- Paper towels (1 or 2 sheets)
- 3 jar lids
- A marker
- 3 resealable plastic bags
- 3 medicine droppers
- 30 radish seeds
- Science notebook
- Motor oil
- A teaspoon
- Laundry detergent
- A ¼ cup measuring cup
- Water
- Aluminum foil
- Ruler

Do you have all of your supplies?

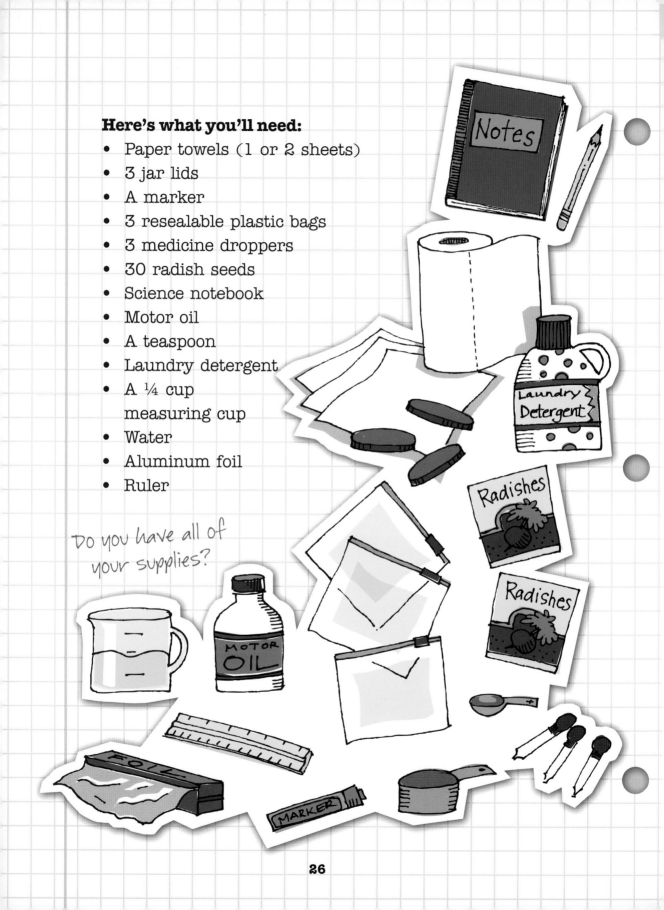

Be careful with the motor oil!

Instructions:

1. Cut the paper towels into a circular shape to fit inside the jar lids. Place one circle in each lid.
2. Using a marker, label each lid "A," "B," and "C." Label each plastic bag "A," "B," and "C."
3. Fill 1 medicine dropper with water. Drip water onto the paper towel in lid A, counting the drops until the towel is fully damp. Write down the number of drops in your science notebook. Place 10 radish seeds, evenly spaced, on the paper towel. Set this lid on bag A.
4. Fill another dropper with motor oil. Ask an adult to help you. Drip the same number of drops you used with lid A onto the paper towel in lid B. Place 10 radish seeds in lid B, spaced as before. Set this lid on bag B.

5. Mix ½ teaspoon laundry detergent with ¼ cup water. Fill the third dropper with the detergent water. Drip the detergent water into lid C. Use the same number of drops that you used for lids A and B. Place 10 radish seeds in lid C. Set lid C on bag C.
6. Carefully wrap each lid with foil. Do not tip the lids over. Place each wrapped lid in its labeled bag, and seal the bags. Set the jar lids aside.
7. After 5 days, remove each lid from the bag and unwrap them. Many of the seeds will have shoots.
8. Count the seeds with shoots, and record the number for each lid in your notebook. Measure the length of the shoots, and record this data for each lid.

Conclusion:

In which lid did the seeds produce the most shoots? In which were the shoots the longest? In which were there the fewest sprouted seeds? How would you explain the seed behavior in each sample? The detergent mixture represents the chemicals and soapsuds that might pollute the environment from washing a car. Can you guess why we used motor oil? What do your results tell you about the impact of pollution on ecosystems?

Experiment #6
Do It Yourself!

We've learned many things from our experiments and observations of ecosystems. So where do you go from here?

You may know from science class that plants turn sunlight into oxygen. Did you know that this is true even in underwater ecosystems?

Can you create an experiment to examine how important sunlight is to a water ecosystem? What is a possible hypothesis? You might want to test this one: **Even under water, green plants need sunlight.** What kind of mini-ecosystem could you create to test this hypothesis?

Studying ecosystems can take you all over the world: to tropical rain forests, deserts, mountain meadows, and even the depths of the ocean. That sounds like a great science adventure!

GLOSSARY

carbon dioxide (KAR-buhn dye-OK-side) a gas that is a mixture of carbon and oxygen

conclusion (kuhn-KLOO-zhuhn) a final decision, thought, or opinion

ecosystems (EE-koh-siss-tuhmz) communities of plants and animals interacting with their environment

ecotone (EE-kuh-tohn) an area between two ecological communities

ethylene (ETH-uh-leen) a gas that speeds the ripening of fruits

hypothesis (hye-POTH-uh-sihss) a logical guess about what will happen in an experiment

method (METH-uhd) a way of doing something

nutrients (NOO-tree-uhntss) things that are needed by plants, animals, and humans to stay healthy

observations (ob-zur-VAY-shuhnz) things that are seen or noticed with one's senses

pesticides (PESS-tuh-sidz) chemicals used to kill insects and other pests

FOR MORE INFORMATION

BOOKS

Davis, Barbara J. *Biomes and Ecosystems*. Milwaukee: Gareth Stevens Publishing, 2007.

Rompella, Natalie. *Ecosystems*. Chicago: Heinemann Library, 2008.

Spilsbury, Louise, and Richard Spilsbury. *The War in Your Backyard: Life in an Ecosystem*. Chicago: Raintree, 2006.

WEB SITES

EcoKids—Wide-Spread Deforestation
www.ecokids.ca/pub/eco_info/topics/forests/deforestation_effects.cfm
Learn how deforestation can harm an ecosystem

Geography4Kids.com—An Ecological System
www.geography4kids.com/files land_ecosystem.html
For information about ecosystems and biomes

PBS—Bill Moyers Reports: Earth on Edge—Ecosystems
www.pbs.org/earthonedge/ecosystems/index.html
Find more information about many ecosystems

INDEX

About the
Author →

Matt Mullins holds a master's degree in the history of science. Matt writes about science and technology, and sometimes about food and wine, culture, and other things that interest him. He lives in Madison, Wisconsin, with his wife and son.